MW00932810

CONTENTS

Introduction

About Ingredients

Flour

There are two kinds of white flour: the all-purpose type used for making breads, cookies, and pies, and cake flour. Use the latter, unless otherwise indicated, for the recipes in this book.

Gelatin

Gelatin must first be soaked in a cold liquid like water or juice before it is added to the hot liquid—the milk or custard—that it is to thicken.

Eggs

Fresh eggs are important to the taste, appearance, and nutrition of your baking. So, buy large eggs in usable quantities, and store them in the refrigerator to preserve their freshness. Remove the number you need and let them come to room temperature when you are baking.

Heavy Cream and Milk

Heavy cream is the fatty part of milk and is often used to make rich cakes and frostings. Milk is more often used in breads, spongecakes, or custards.

Butter

There is salted and unsalted (or, "sweet") butter, and the AA code denotes the best quality. Use salted butter for cooking unless otherwise indicated. Store it well wrapped in the refrigerator, and remove 30 minutes before mixing.

Leavenings

Baking powder or baking soda are the fast-rising agents most frequently used in cakes. Store them away from moisture and, when using, measure the quantity exactly and sift with the flour two or three times before mixing with liquid ingredients.

Sugar

There is granulated, brown, and confectioners' sugar. The latter, also called powdered sugar, is most used to frost and decorate cakes, while brown is most often used in breads. Store each carefully to keep them from getting lumpy and hard.

Flavorings

Juices and rinds, extracts and liqueurs add delicate flavors to your cakes. Only a few drops are usually needed, so measure carefully, according to your recipe.

Terms for Cake Making

...corations

...ilver Dragées ... Small silver ...y balls. **2. Candied Angelica**... ...died sugar cane. **3. Candied** ...osa ... Candied petals of mimosa. ...andied Cherries **5. Canned** ...ries **6. Marzipan** ... Almond ...e with confectioners' sugar. ...ed with food colorings, it can be ...e into small flowers or fruits for ...rations.

...od Colorings

...d coloring, which comes in red, ...w, blue, and green, is handy to ... Peppermint (green), grenadine ...o (red), powdered green tea, and ...a are used, too. Be careful not ...se too much of though!

...ts and Dried Fruits

...onds, walnuts, peanuts or ...chio nuts are often used. Sliced ...chopped nuts are available. ...ns and dried apricots are also ...lar. Use them for garnish as ...as for mixing with batter.

...ocolates and Jams

...r chocolate (cooking chocolate) ...sweet chocolate are used. There ...many kinds of jams available. ...ts smoothness, apricot jam is ...u used for glazing.

1. **Strain** ..... Press ingredients through a sieve to make them smooth. Lumps or fibers can be removed.
2. **Batter (dough)** ..... The mixture of flour, butter, and eggs is called batter (dough, when it is hard enough to work with the hands) before it is baked or cooked.
3. **Place in ice water** ..... To chill immediately, place a bowl of ingredients in a larger bowl of ice water.
4. **Beat until stiff peaks form** ..... Beat egg whites or heavy cream until stiff peaks form when beater is raised.
5. **Meringue** ..... Egg whites with beaten sugar. Use fresh eggs to make a good meringue.
6. **Purée** ..... To press fruits or vegetables through a sieve and make smooth soup or sauce.
7. **Whip** ..... To beat egg whites, heavy cream, etc., rapidly.
8. **Rest** ..... When batter or dough for cakes or cookies is placed it in the refrigerator to rest for 20 to 30 minutes, which lets the ingredients blend and develop flavor.
9. **Cook in a double boiler** ..... Place saucepan in larger saucepan filled with boiling water to cook or keep food warm. A double boiler is also often used for melting butter or cooking sauces.

Control heat carefully according to the recipe. If there is no comment about heat level, cook over MEDIUM HEAT.

Utensils

Measurements

Cake ingredients must be measured exactly. A large glass measuring cup, plus a set of graduated cups for leveling, make good basic equipment, and it is also necessary to have a set of graduated measuring spoons.

Sifters and Strainers

Flour, sugar, and any other powdered ingredients need to be sifted before use, so purchase a sifter of good quality and convenient size. A regular strainer can be used for a decorative dusting of powdered sugar over the finished cake.

Mixers

Food processors and standard and portable electric mixers bring new conveniences to the cook, and are valuable adjuncts to the wire whisk and mixing bowl.

Wooden Spoon, Brush and Scraper

Wooden spoons are useful for mixing, stirring, or folding in ingredients. A pastry brush of good quality is useful for spreading melted butter or diluted jam over cakes. A rubber spatula is a convenient tool for scraping.

Saucepans & Steamer

A 2-quart saucepan is the most convenient all-purpose size to use. Choose one of good quality with a heavy base. A big, square steamer is useful; a fine-holed rack is the best conductor of heat in one.

Various Pans and Cutters

Springform

Loaf Pan

Pudding Cup

Doughnut Cutter

Cookie Cu

Brioche mold   Gelatin Molds   Heart-shaped

Pastry Bags and Tips

Choose a pastry bag that is easy to use. Beginners will find the tip with the large cut-out easiest, and the round and star tips are also used often. To write letters, make a cone shape with wax paper and cut off the point.

Lemon Squeezer

Lemon juice is often used in cake-making. Cut lemon in half, place half-lemon on a citrus squeezer and press. Use juice, omitting seeds and fibers. Choose a juicy lemon.

Check the Following Before You Start!

Wear apron.

Wash your hands.

Read the recipe and directions carefully.

Don't change the order of blending.

Measure all ingredients exactly.

×

Prepare the utensils and ingredients you need before you start.

Clean up after cooking.

Now, let's start!

Yogurt Gelatin

Variation:

Yogurt Gelatin with Fruits

Ingredients: **several kinds of fruit you like:** Strawberries;
Pineapples; Kiwi fruits. **Yogurt Gelatin.**
If you don't have a gelatin mold, pour gelatin mixture
into glasses and chill until firm. You may add fruits in
season for a colorful gelatin cocktail.

ngredients for 4 servings. 2 teaspoons unflavored gelatin
nd 2 tablespoons water; 1/2 cup unsweetened yogurt;
cup milk; 1/2 cup sugar; 4 teaspoons lemon juice.
or A: 2 teaspoons liqueur; 4 sections of canned mandarins.
or B: 2 teaspoons peppermint; 1 slice kiwi fruit
or C: 2 teaspoons grenadine syrup; 1 strawberry.

Utensils

1

Gelatin

2 tablespoons water

prinkle gelatin over 2 tablespoons
ater in bowl and let it soak for 2 to
minutes.

2

Sugar   Milk

Combine milk and sugar in small
saucepan and heat to 165°F-185°F
(just before it starts bubbling).

3

Softened gelatin

185°F milk
and sugar

Add softened gelatin and stir to
dissolve. Set aside to cool.

4

Yogurt

Lemon juice

fter it cools, stir in yogurt and
mon juice.

5

Ⓐ   Liqueur

Ⓑ   Ⓒ

Peppermint   Grenadine
              syrup

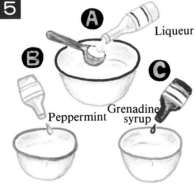

Divide yogurt mixture into 4 parts—
2 for A, 1 each for B and C. Add indicated flavors to A, B, and C.

6

Spoon into 4 wet molds; refrigerate
until firm.

Dip molds

Lukewarm water

ip molds in lukewarm water and
vert onto serving dishes. Garnish
ith fruits.

For Yogurt Gelatin with Fruits

Ice water

Place bowl of yogurt mixture in ice
water to chill and thicken. Add fruits
to mixture and refrigerate until firm.

**Note: How to unmold gelatin des-
serts onto dishes.**

Choose dishes match that desserts
and cool them before use. Dip them
in cold water for a second to prevent
sticking. You may garnish with leaves
or flowers in season instead of using
whipped cream.

Blanc Mange

Variation:

Coffee Blanc Mange

Ingredients:
l tablespoon instant coffee.
For Coffee Sauce:
1 cup water; 3 tablespoons sugar; 1 tablespoon instant coffee;
1 teaspoon cornstarch.
Other ingredients are the same as Blanc Mange.
The coffee sauce is poured over it for this tasty variation.

Ingredients for 5 servings. 2-1/4 cups milk; 5 tablespoons cornstarch; 8 tablespoons sugar; Vnailla xtract. For Garnish: 5 canned plums; 5 canned yellow peaches (halved). For Apricot sauce: 2 tablespoons apricot jam; 4 tablespoons syrup eserved from canned fruits.

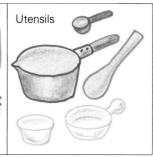

Utensils

1

Sugar
Cornstarch
Milk
Stir

n saucepan, combine sugar and ornstarch; add milk and stir.

2

Vanilla
Don't scorch

Heat, stirring constantly until it reaches a smooth and creamy texture, for 2 to 3 minutes.

3

Pour into five dishes while it is hot. (When cool, it becomes too firm to pour.)

4

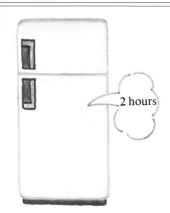

2 hours

efrigerate for about 2 hours until rm.

5

Plums
Yellow peaches

Garnish with yellow peaches and plums.

6

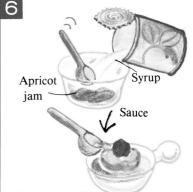

Apricot jam
Syrup
Sauce

Make sauce with reserved syrup and apricot jam. Pour sauce over Blanc Mange.

For Coffee Blanc Mange

Sugar
ornstarch
Instant coffee
ilk
Heat and stir

Add instant coffee to ingredients f Blanc Mange. Heat and stir as in teps 1 and 2.

2

Pour mixture into 5 molds; refrigerate until firm.

3

Coffee sauce
Water
Sugar
Instant coffee
Cornstarch
Chill

Make coffee sauce and chill. Pour over Coffee Blanc Mange.

Custard Pudding

Variation:

Pudding à la Mode
Ingredients:
Whipped cream;
Canned pineapples, yellow peaches, and cherries.
Don't be disappointed if they don't turn out absolutely
perfect the first time. Practice, and you'll enjoy the
taste of home-made pudding.

ngredients for 10 puddings. For Caramel Syrup: 1 cup ugar; 2/5 cup water; 2 tablespoons boiling water. 6 large ggs; 3 cups milk; 1 cup sugar: Vanilla extract; Rum or dry herry.

Utensils

1

Sugar

Caramel syrup

Water

Make caramel syrup. Place sugar nd water in saucepan and cook ntil sugar forms a brown syrup.

2

2 tablespoons boiling water

Shake saucepan without stirring. Add boiling water after removing from heat. Shake saucepan to mix.

3

Pour syrup into 10 custard cups while it is hot. Let cool.

4

Sugar

165°F-185°F

Milk

Combine milk and sugar in saucepan nd heat to 165°F-185°F.

5

Egg

In large bowl, beat eggs lightly with wire whisk.

6

Milk

Pour in hot milk gradually, stirring constantly.

7

Sieve

Rum or dry sherry

nilla

train egg mixture to make it smooth. dd vanilla and rum or dry sherry.

8

Place cups on a rack in hot steamer.

Stick

Dishcloth

Place the lid

Medium heat

Steam over medium heat for about 30 to 40 minutes, placing the lid as shown.

For Pudding á la Mode

Whipped cream

Pineapples

Yellow peaches

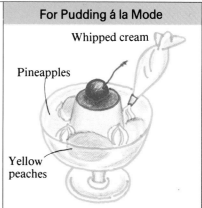

Garnish pudding with whipped cream (see page 47) and colorful fruits.

11

Cheesecake

Ingredients for 9-inch cheesecake or 8 servings. 2 teaspoons unflavored gelatin and 3 tablespoons water; 3/4 cup cream cheese; 3/4 cup plain yogurt; 1 cup heavy cream; 2 tablespoons lemon juice; 6 tablespoons sugar. For Meringue: 1 egg white; 1 tablespoon sugar. For decoration and topping: Ribbon; Raspberry jam.

Egg white

Utensils

Springform pan

1

Hot water
Cream cheese

Soften cream cheese, placing bowl in hot water.

2

Sugar
Lemon juice

Beat cream cheese. Add 6 tablespoons sugar and lemon juice. Beat until smooth and well mixed.

3

Heavy cream

In bowl, beat heavy cream until foamy and stir in cream cheese mixture.

4

Gelatin
Water
Hot water

In small bowl, sprinkle gelatin over 3 tablespoons water. Place the bowl in hot water to dissolve gelatin. Add softened gelatin to cream cheese mixture.

5

Yogurt

Stir in yogurt.

6

Egg white
Sugar
Meringue

Beat egg white until foamy. Add sugar and beat until stiff. Fold in yogurt mixture.

7

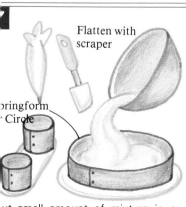
Flatten with scraper
Springform
Circle

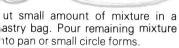

Put small amount of mixture in a pastry bag. Pour remaining mixture into pan or small circle forms.

8

Decorate top as shown or with desired design. Refrigerate for about 2 hours until firm.

9

Raspberry jam
Ribbon

Place warm cloth around circle and remove cake. Tie ribbon as shown. Spread jam over small cakes.

Bavarian Cream

Chocolate Bavarian Cream

Bavarian Cream

Bavarian Cream

Ingredients for 5 servings.
2 teaspoons unflavored gelatin and 2 tablespoons water; 1 cup milk; 2 egg yolks; 1/2 cup heavy cream; 1/2 cup sugar; Vanilla extract; Grenadine syrup.
For Garnish:
Whipped cream; Marzipan Roses.

Chocolate Bavarian Cream

Ingredients for 5 servings.
1 tablespoon chocolate; other ingredients are same as Bavarian Cream.
For Garnish:
Whipped cream; Chocolate cookies.

1

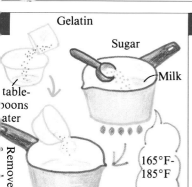

Gelatin
Sugar
Milk
2 tablespoons water
Remove
165°F-185°F

Combine sugar and milk in saucepan and heat to 165°F-185°F. Add softened gelatin and stir to dissolve.

2

Egg yolks

In bowl, beat egg yolks lightly and pour gelatin mixture gradually into egg yolks.

3

Strain mixture to make it smooth.

4

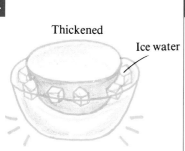

Thickened
Ice water

Place bowl in larger bowl of ice water and chill until mixture is thickened.

5

Grenadine
Heavy cream
Vanilla

Beat heavy cream, vanilla, and grenadine syrup until foamy, placing bowl in ice water. Fold whipped cream into gelatin mixture.

6

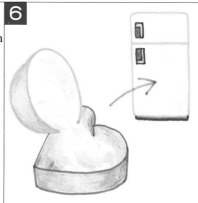

Turn into a wet mold and refrigerate until firm.

7

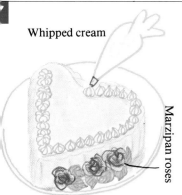

Whipped cream
Marzipan roses

Invert onto serving plate and garnish with whipped cream (see page 47) and marzipan roses.

For Chocolate Bavarian Cream

1

Chocolate
Sugar and milk
Softened gelatin

In saucepan, combine milk and sugar. Heat to 165°F-185°F. Add chocolate and stir to melt.
Then add softened gelatin. Following directions above, make Chocolate Bavarian Cream.

2

Chocolate cookies
Whipped cream

After refrigerating until firm, invert into individual glass and garnish with whipped cream and chocolate cookies.

Oeufs à la Neige (or Eggs in Snow)

Ingredients for 6 servings.
1-1/4 cups milk; 3 egg whites and 2/3 cup sugar for meringue.
For Garnish:
Slivered, toasted almonds.
For Chocolate sauce: 4 teaspoons chocolate.
For Custard sauce: 2 egg yolks; 3 tablespoons sugar; 1 teaspoon flour; 1 cup milk (used to poach meringue); Vanilla extract; Dry sherry.

Utensils

1

Egg whites

Clean bowl

In bowl, beat egg whites.

2

Sugar

Add sugar by halves

Add sugar by halves. Beat.

3

Continue to beat until stiff peaks form.

4

Orange-sized

165°F-185°F milk

Heat milk to 165°F-185°F. Drop meringue, forming an orange-sized ball, in hot milk. Poach for about 1 to 2 minutes and turn them.

5

Place them on a wire rack or sieve to drain. Strain hot milk to make custard sauce.

6

Flour

Sugar

Custard sauce

Egg yolks

Milk (milk used to poach meringues)

Make sauce by combining egg yolks, sugar, and flour in saucepan.

7

Vanilla

Sherry

Pour in strained milk, stirring constantly. Add vanilla and sherry.

8

Chocolate

Chocolate sauce

Hot water

One-third of custard sauce

Make chocolate sauce. Place one-third of custard sauce in bowl. Add melted chocolate to custard and mix well.

9

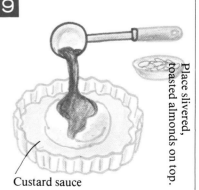

Place slivered, toasted almonds on top.

Custard sauce

Pour custard in serving dish, place meringue in it and pour chocolate sauce over it.

Strawberry Mousse

Variation:

Lemon Mousse
If strawberries are not available, make Lemon Mousse. Nobody can refuse the refreshing flavor of lemon.

Strawberry Mousse

Ingredients for 8 servings.
2 teaspoons unflavored gelatin and 1/4 cup water; 7 ounces strawberries; 1 cup heavy cream; 1 tablespoon lemon juice; 11 tablespoons sugar.
For Meringue:
2 eggs whites; 2 tablespoons sugar.
For Garnish: Whipped cream; Strawberries; Pistachio nuts.

For Lemon Mousse

Ingredients for 8 servings.
2 teaspoons unflavored gelatin and 1/5 cup water; 1/2 cup lemon juice; 1 cup heavy cream; 1 cup sugar; 1/2 cup water.
For Meringue: 2 egg whites; 2 tablespoons sugar.
For Garnish:
Chocolate cookies; Pistachio nuts; Lemon slices.

1

Wash strawberries and drain. Press them through a sieve to make a purée.

2

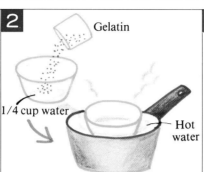

Gelatin

1/4 cup water

Hot water

Sprinkle gelatin over water. Set aside for 2 to 3 minutes to soften. Place bowl in hot water to dissolve gelatin.

3

Softened gelatin

Lemon juice

Sugar

Add sugar and lemon juice to strawberry purée; stir to blend. Stir in softened gelatin.

4

Heavy cream

Thicken

Ice water

Place bowl in ice water to thicken gelatin mixture. Beat heavy cream until foamy and fold in gelatin mixture.

5

Sugar

Egg whites

Meringue

Beat egg whites, gradually adding sugar and beat until stiff peaks form. Fold in cream and gelatin mixture.

6

Pour in a serving dish, mounding.

7

Hull and soak in hot water

Pistachio nuts

Strawberry

Whipped cream

Refrigerate for about 2 hours until firm. Garnish with whipped cream, halved strawberries and pistachio nuts.

Lemon Mousse

1

Sugar

Softened gelatin

Syrup

Lemon juice

In saucepan, combine water and sugar. Heat to make syrup. Add lemon juice and softened gelatin. Stir to dissolve gelatin.

2

Lemon mousse

Garnish with lemon and pistachio nuts

Chocolate cookies

Fold whipped cream and meringue in gelatin mixture in same way as in steps 3 and 4. Refrigerate to chill. Garnish with lemon and pistachio nuts.

Fruit Gelatins

Make basic clear gelatin. Then add your favorite fruits and flavors.

A Yellow peaches
B Strawberries
C Mandarins
D Oranges
E Grenadine
F Lemon
G Peppermint

Ingredients for 4 servings or 8 cups.
For Basic Gelatin: 3 teaspoons unflavored gelatin and 5 tablespoons water; 3/4 cup sugar; 1 tablespoon lemon juice; 2 cups water.

A Yellow Peach Gelatin- 4 servings.
4 slices canned peaches; 4 teaspoons peppermint; 4 teaspoons liqueur.

B Strawberry Gelatin-4 servings.
10-15 strawberries; 4 teaspoons grenadine syrup; 4 teaspoons liqueur.

C Mandarin Gelatin: Mandarins (canned); 4 teaspoons peppermint.

D Orange Gelatin: Substitute 2 cups orange juice for water when making basic gelatin.

E Grenadine Gelatin: Add 8 teaspoons grenadine syrup to basic gelatin.

F Lemon Gelatin: Add 4 teaspoons lemon juice and 4 teaspoons liqueur to basic gelatin.

G Peppermint Gelatin: Add 8 teaspoons peppermint to basic gelatin.

1

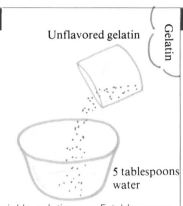

Unflavored gelatin · Gelatin
5 tablespoons water

Sprinkle gelatin over 5 tablespoons water and let it soak for about 2 to 3 minutes.

2

Sugar
2 cups water

In saucepan, place water and sugar. Heat to 165°F-185°F and stir to dissolve sugar.

3

Softened gelatin

Remove from heat. Stir in softened gelatin to dissolve.

4

Lemon juice
Ice water

Place saucepan in ice water to cool and add lemon juice to make basic gelatin.

5

(a) Peppermint
Liqueur (b) Peach

Divide basic gelatin into two. Add peppermint to (a) and liqueur to (b).

6

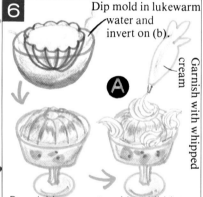

Dip mold in lukewarm water and invert on (b).
Garnish with whipped cream
A

Pour (a) into a wet mold and (b) into a glass with sliced peaches. Refrigerate until firm.

---

7 Make basic gelatin following steps 1 through 4. Divide basic gelatin

Grenadine
Strawberry
Liqueur
B

nto two. Add grenadine syrup to (a) and liqueur to (b). Chill. Garnish with whipped cream (see page 47).

C Mandarin Gelatin

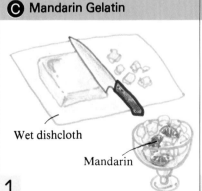

Wet dishcloth
Mandarin

1 Chill basic gelatin with peppermint. Mix chopped peppermint gelatin and mandarins. Place in serving dish.

D E F G

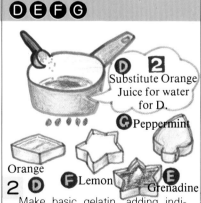

D 2 Substitute Orange Juice for water for D.
G Peppermint
Orange
F Lemon
E Grenadine

2 D Make basic gelatin, adding indicated ingredients. Pour in individual molds and chill.

Ice Creams

Variation:

Ice Cream Sundae

Ingredients:
Cherries, pineapples, canned peaches, vanilla and strawberry ice cream, and whipped cream.

A. Vanilla Ice Cream

Ingredients for 5-6 servings.
4 egg yolks; 1-1/4 cups sugar; 1 tablespoon cornstarch; 2 cups milk; 1 cup heavy cream; Vanilla extract and desired liqueur.

B. Cocoa Ice Cream

Same ingredients as Vanilla ice cream plus A tablespoons cocoa.

C. Strawberry Ice Cream

Same ingredients as Vanilla ice cream plus 7 ounces strawberries.

1

Warm milk
Cornstarch
Egg yolks
One-half at a time
Sugar

In saucepan, combine egg yolks, warm milk, sugar, and cornstarch and stir to blend well.

2

Cook until slightly thickened.

3

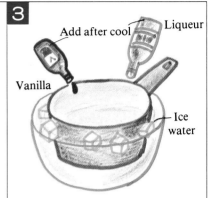

Add after cool
Liqueur
Vanilla
Ice water

Remove from heat. Place saucepan in ice water to cool. Add vanilla and desired liqueur.

4

Heavy cream
Ice water
Thickened

Whip cream placing bowl in ice water. Fold whipped cream into egg yolk mixture.

5

Becomes firm fast in metal pan

Pour in metal pan. Place pan in freezer.

6

Repeat 3 or 4 times to make a smooth texture.

When mixture becomes firm, stir with spoon. Flatten surface and return to freezer.

B

Milk
Cornstarch
Sugar
Egg yolks
Dissolved in hot water
Cocoa milk

Make in same manner as for A, but add dissolved cocoa to warm milk.

C

Press strawberries through a sieve to make a purée. Add to egg yolk

Strawberries

mixture. Follow steps 4 through 6 as for A.

For Ice Cream Sundae

Pineapple
Cherry
Whipped cream
Strawberry ice cream
Peach
Vanilla ice cream

Place your favorite ice cream and fruits in serving glass and garnish with whipped cream.

Sherbets

Variation:

Make fancy drinks, adding sherbets to soda or cider.

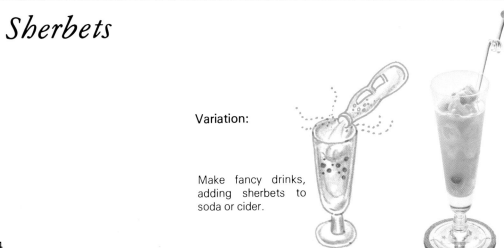

Egg white

A

Lemon Sherbet

3/4 cup sugar; 1/4 cup lemon juice; 1-1/4 cups water; 2 teaspoons curaçao.

For Meringue:
1/3 egg white; 1 tablespoon sugar. 4 slices of lemon.

B

Orange Sherbet
(4 servings)

Sugar (Adjust amount of sugar to sweetness of juice.) 1/2 cup orange juice; 1 tablespoon lemon juice; 1 cup water; 2 teaspoons liqueur.

For Meringue: Same as A.

C

Strawberry Sherbet
(4 servings)

5/6 cup sugar; 10 ounces strawberries; 1 tablespoon lemon juice.

For Meringue: Same as A.

1

A

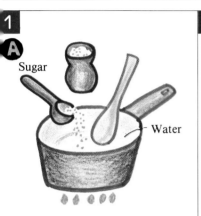

Sugar

Water

Place water and sugar in saucepan. Heat and stir to dissolve sugar.

2

Ice water

Place saucepan in ice water to cool.

3

Lemon juice   Curaçao

Add lemon juice and liqueur.

4

Pour in metal pan and place pan in freezer.

5

Repeat this 3 or 4 times.

Stir until like sleet

Remove pan from freezer and stir with spoon and return to freezer again. Repeat this 3 or 4 times.

6

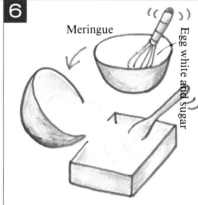

Meringue

Egg white and sugar

Make meringue. Fold meringue into half-frozen juice mixture.

7

Garnish with lemon slice

Return to freezer again to be frozen. Remove from freezer and spoon sherbet in serving dish. Garnish with lemon slice.

B   Orange Sherbet

Orange juice   Lemon juice   Liqueur

Fold in meringue mixture.

Make in same manner as for A. Add sugar depending on sweetness of juice.

C   Strawberry Sherbet

Make a purée, pressing strawberries
Strawberries
Lemon juice   Sugar

Fold in meringue mixture.

through a sieve. Substitute purée for water. Make in same manner as for A.

25

Shortcake

Variation:

Apricot Cake

Using same ingredients as for spongecake, this is made in a square and garnished with apricots and whipped cream. Use canned peaches and cherries. To decorate cakes, use big tips and simple designs. When experienced, you may use various kinds of tips. Don't overdecorate cakes.

Strawberry Shortcake

Ingredients for 8-inch shortcake.
For Batter:
3 large eggs; 1 cup sugar; 1 cup flour; 1 tablespoon milk; 1 tablespoon butter.
For Whipped Cream:
1 cup heavy cream; 2 tablespoons sugar; Vanilla extract and desired liqueur. Strawberries.

Apricot Cake

Ingredients for 6-inch square cake.
Same ingredients as strawberry shortcake except for strawberries.
For Garnish:
Canned apricots and candied angelica.

1

Sugar — Eggs

Beat until foamy

In bowl, beat eggs and sugar until foamy.

2

Sifter

Flour

Fold in sifted flour.

3

Butter — Hot water

Milk

Fold in milk and melted butter.

4

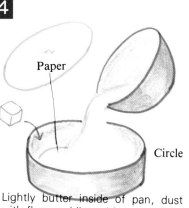

Paper

Circle

Lightly butter inside of pan, dust with flour and line with paper. Pour batter into pan.

5

Dishcloth

Place pan on a rack in a hot steamer. Steam over high heat for about 25 to 30 minutes.

6

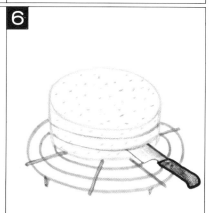

Invert steamed cake on wire rack to cool. Slice cake across into 3 layers.

7

Spread whipped cream over each

Whipped cream

Strawberry

layer. Place halved strawberries over whipped cream. Place three layers together.

8

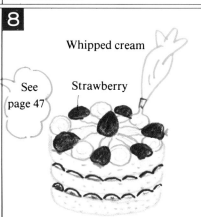

Whipped cream

See page 47

Strawberry

Garnish top with whipped cream and strawberries.

For Apricot Cake

Make square shortcake. Slice across

Whipped cream

Apricots

Angelica

cake and spread with whipped cream and sliced apricots. Garnish with whipped cream, apricots, and candied angelica.

Birthday Cake

Ⓐ Birthday Cake:

Ingredients for 8-inch spongecake.
Make same batter as Shortcake on page 2.
For Butter Cream:
5/6 cup unsalted butter; 6 tablespoons sugar; 5 teaspoons water; Vanilla extract and liqueur. Red food coloring. Cocoa.
For Garnish:
Silver dragées; Confetti.

Ⓑ Chocolate Cake:

Ingredients for one loaf.
For Batter:
2 eggs; 1/2 cup sugar; 1/2 cup flour; 1/2 tablespoon milk; 1/2 tablespoon butter; 1 tablespoon cocoa.
For Chocolate Butter Cream:
5/6 cup unsalted butter; 4 tablespoons sugar; 5 teaspoons water; 3 tablespoons chocolate.
For Garnish:
Cherries; Confectioners' sugar; Chocolate.

1

Sugar · Butter cueam · 5 teaspoons water

In saucepan, combine water and sugar. Heat to make syrup. Remove from heat and let cool completely.

2

Let cool completely. · Syrup · Butter

Cream butter. Stir in syrup.

3

Vanilla · Liqueur · Water · Red food coloring · For letters · Cocoa

Add vanilla, liqueur and red food coloring. For letters, add cocoa to make brown cream.

4

Make spongecake, following direc-

Butter cream

tions on page 27. Slice across cake in half. Spread butter cream all over top and side.

5

Using pastry bag, decorate cake with pink butter cream as shown.

Butter cream (Pink) · Butter cream (Brown) · HAPPY BIRTHDA · Silver dragées · Confetti

Write letters with brown butter cream. Garnish with silver dragées and confetti.

For Chocolate Cake

1

Make spongecake in same manner as shown on page 27. Slice cake into three layers.

2

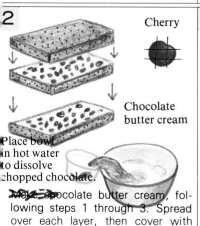

Cherry · Chocolate butter cream · Place bowl in hot water to dissolve chopped chocolate.

Make chocolate butter cream, following steps 1 through 3. Spread over each layer, then cover with chopped cherries.

3

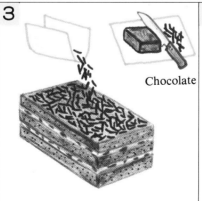

Chocolate

Sprinkle chopped chocolate over top.

4

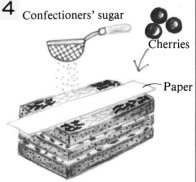

Confectioners' sugar · Cherries · Paper

Place a strip of paper across top before sprinkling with confectioners' sugar. Garnish with cherries.

29

Sweet Breads

Variation:

Toast with Strawberries
Ingredients (makes 1 serving)
1 slice bread; 6-8 strawberries; 1 tablespoon sugar; Butter
Liqueur; Whipped cream (see page 47).

Ingredients for 3 servings.
6 slices bread.
For Garnish:
Apricot jam; Strawberry jam; Powdered green tea.
For Custard:
2 egg yolks; 1 cup milk; 2 tablespoons flour; 1/3
cup sugar; Vanilla extract; Brandy.

Utensils

1

Using cookie cutters, cut two of each shape from bread. Toast them.

2

Sugar

Custard

Flour

Hot milk

Egg yolks

In saucepan, combine egg yolks, sugar, and flour. Mix well. Pour in hot milk gradually.

3

Liqueur

Vanilla

Let cool

Cook to thicken. Let cool. Add vanilla and brandy.

4

Custard cream

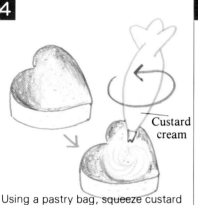

Using a pastry bag, squeeze custard cream over toasted bread. Place matching toasted bread over it.

5

Jam
● Strawberry
● Apricot
● Powdered green tea

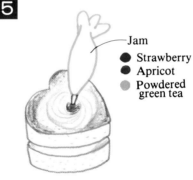

Garnish tops with custard cream and jam.

6

Knead powdered green tea in hot water.

Apricot jam

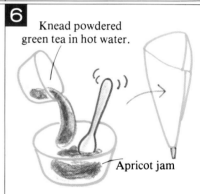

To make green jam, mix dissolved, powdered green tea with apricot jam.

Toast with strawberries

1

Brandy

Sugar

Sprinkle sugar and liqueur over strawberries. Press them with spoon.

2

Spread butter over toast. Place

Butter

Strawberries

Whipped cream

pressed strawberries on toast and pour whipped cream over strawberries.

Note:
To butter cake pan.
Cream butter. Then apply butter carefully to cake pan, using brush or fingers. Refrigerate to cool. Remove from refrigerator and dust with flour lightly. Pour batter in prepared pan. Use good (AA) butter.

Ingredients for 5 servings.
25 ready-made rectangular biscuits.
For Garnish:
Candied mimosa; Silver dragées.
Milk to soak biscuits.
For Whipped Cream:
1 cup heavy cream; 3 tablespoons sugar; Vanilla extract; Desired liqueur; 1 tablespoon cocoa, 1 teaspoon each of sugar and hot water.

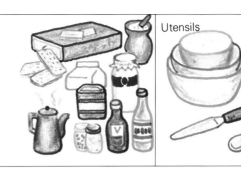

Utensils

1

Brandy Vanilla

Sugar

Heavy cream

Ice water

Combine heavy cream, sugar, vanilla, and desired liqueur in bowl. Whip, placing bowl in ice water.

2

Boiling water

Sugar

Cocoa

In small bowl, mix cocoa, sugar, and boiling water. Stir to blend.

3

Cocoa mixture

1

Whipped cream

Add dissolved cocoa to whipped cream to make light brown cream.

4

Biscuits

Milk

Dip biscuits in milk.

5

Whipped cream and dissolved cocoa

Repeat until there are 5 layers.

Place 5 biscuits in row and spread cream mixture over biscuits. Repeat until there are 5 layers.

6

Silver dragées

Mimosa

Over the whipped cream mixture, sprinkle the candied mimosa and silver dragées. Chill unitl firm.

Note:
Variations made of biscuits.

You may turn ordinary ready-made biscuits into fancy desserts.
Use plain biscuits, not sweet or salty.

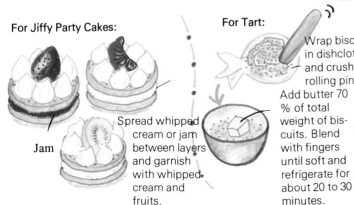

For Jiffy Party Cakes:

Jam

Spread whipped cream or jam between layers and garnish with whipped cream and fruits.

For Tart:

Wrap biscuits in dishcloth and crush with rolling pin. Add butter 70 % of total weight of biscuits. Blend with fingers until soft and refrigerate for about 20 to 30 minutes.

Press chilled crumbs on bottom and side of pie plate. Fill with whipped cream and fruits. Chill in the refrigerator.

Crumbs

Pie plate

For Ice Cream Sticks:

Mix crushed biscuits and ice cream well. Form into sticks and wrap each stick in plastic film. Freeze.

Fruit Sandwiches

Variation:

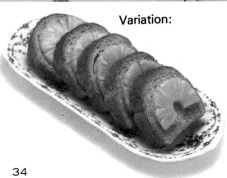

Rye Bread Open Sandwich

Ingredients for 5 servings. 5 slices rye bread; 2/3 cup sugar; 1 cup water and 4 teaspoons brandy for syrup; 5 slices canned pineapples; Apricot jam.

Enjoy slight bitter taste of rye bread with the flavor of brandy. Substitute juice or syrup for brandy for children. Chill before you eat.

Ingredients for 4-5 servings.
2 pounds bread.
For Meringue:
2 egg whites; 5/6 cup sugar; Vanilla extract.
Strawberries. Kiwi fruits. Canned mandarin oranges.
For Garnish:
Slivered toasted almonds.

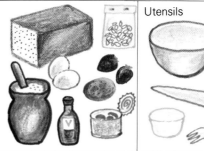

Utensils

1

Egg whites

Place egg whites in clean dry bowl and beat.

2

Sugar

One-half at a time

Beat egg whites until foamy, then add sugar.

3

Vanilla

Continue to beat until stiff peaks form when beater is raised. Add vanilla.

4

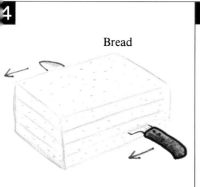

Bread

Cut off crusts of bread. Slice across into 4 lengths.

5

Meringue

Strawberry

Spread with meringue and the sliced strawberries. Place bread on it.

6

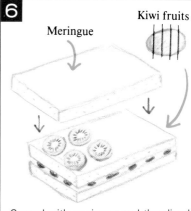

Meringue

Kiwi fruits

Spread with meringue and the sliced kiwi fruits. Place bread on it.

7

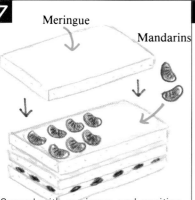

Meringue

Mandarins

Spread with meringue and position the drained mandarins. Place bread on it.

8

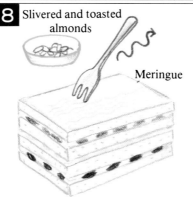

Slivered and toasted almonds

Meringue

Spread with meringue and make wave patterns with a fork. Sprinkle with slivered and toasted almonds.

For Rye Open Sandwich

Brandy

Sugar and water

Apricot jam

Pineapple

Make syrup and pour it over bread. Place sliced pineapple on it and chill.

Butter Cake

Raisin Butter Cake

Marble Cake

Cupcakes
Use same ingredients for cupcakes as for cakes. Ingredients for one loaf make six cupcakes. Brush apricot jam on tops and sides. Cover with chopped nuts and garnish with fruits in season.

Raisin Butter Cake

Ingredients for 1 loaf.
For Batter: 1/2 cup butter: 3/4 cup sugar; 2 eggs; 2 ounces raisins; 1-1/5 cups flour; 1/3 teaspoon baking powder. Apricot jam.   For Garnish:
Apricot jam, Nuts, Candied cherries and angelica.

Marble Cake

Ingredients:
Same ingredients as Raisin Butter Cake.
To make Cocoa Batter (1 tablespoon):
1 tablespoon cocoa and sugar; 1 teaspoon boiling water.

Utensils

1

Add sugar, One-half or one-third at a time.

Cream butter

Cream butter and add sugar, one-half or one-third at a time. Beat well.

2

Eggs

Gradually stir in eggs and beat.

3

Chopped raisins

Add chopped raisins and mix with wooden spoon.

4

Flour

Sift

Baking powder

Sift flour with baking powder over butter mixture and fold.

5

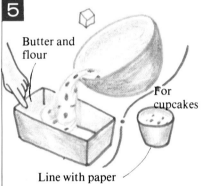

Butter and flour

For cupcakes

Line with paper

Butter and flour a loaf pan, line with paper, and pour batter into pan.

6

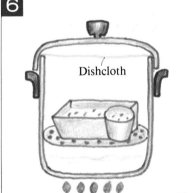

Dishcloth

Place pan on rack in a steamer with boiling water. Steam over high heat for about 25 or 30 minutes.

---

7 Remove cake from pan and brush apricot jam over it.

Brush with apricot jam and chopped nuts.

Cherry

Angelica

For cupcakes, cover with chopped nuts. Garnish with candied cherries and angelica.

For Marble Cake **1**

Flour   Baking powder

Stir lightly

Place one fifth of batter.   **1~2**

Cocoa mixture

Cocoa and sugar in boiling water

Make batter (steps 1, 2, 4) and place one-fifth of batter in bowl. Add dissolved cocoa, mix well.

Dot cocoa mixture onto plain batter. Stir lightly. **2**

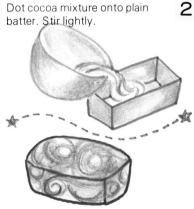

Butter and flour loaf pan and line with paper. Pour in batter and steam.

Vegetable Muffins

Ingredients for 10 muffins.
4 tablespoons butter; 6 tablespoons sugar; 2 eggs;
1/2 cup milk; 1-4/5 cups flour; 1/2 tablespoon
baking powder; 3-1/2 ounces vegetables (diced
carrots, green peas and whole kernel corn).
For Quick Consomme (1 serving)
1 bouillon cube; Dash of salt and pepper; Small
amount each of minced parsley, bread, and butter;
1 cup water.

Utensils

1

Add sugar

Cream butter. Add sugar, a half or third at a time. Beat until light and fluffy.

2

Beaten eggs

Gradually add eggs and beat.

3

Green peas
Kernel corn   Diced carrots

Cook vegetables, drain, and mix into butter mixture with a wooden spoon.

4

1/4 cup milk

Stir in 1/4 cup milk warmed to room temperature.

5

Flour   Baking powder

1/4 cup milk

Fold in flour sifted with baking powder and remaining milk.

6

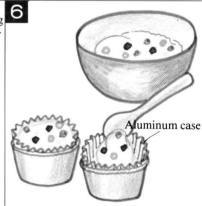

Aluminum case

Line cups with aluminum cases. Spoon mixture into individual cups.

7

Place cups on a rack in a steamer with boiling water. Steam over high heat for about 25 or 30 minutes.

For Quick Consommé

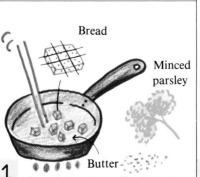

Bread

Minced parsley

Butter

1 Cut bread into dice. Sauté in hot butter until light brown to make croûtons.

Dissolve bouillon cube in hot water

Bouillon cube   Salt

Water   Croûtons Parsley

2 and pour it into serving dish. Add croûtons and minced parsley to hot soup.

Fried Cream Puffs

Ingredients for 15 Cream Puffs.
For Dough:
5 tablespoons butter; 6 tablespoons water; 3/4 cup flour; 3-1/2 eggs.
Confectioners' sugar. Salad oil or shortening for frying.
For Custard Filling:
3 egg yolks; 1/2 cup sugar; 3 tablespoons flour; 1-1/2 cups milk; Vanilla extract.

Utensils

1

Butter and water

Combine water and butter in saucepan. Heat to melt butter and bring to boiling.

2

Sifted flour

Stir one minute

Add sifted flour quickly and stir for one minute.

3

Add lightly beaten eggs, one-third at a time

Beaten eggs

Remove from heat. Gradually add lightly beaten eggs, one-third at a time, making sure the dough is not too thin.

4

55°F

Oil

Spoon dough into hot oil, making round shape.

5

Fry until lightly browned and puffed. Drain on a wire rack.

6

Warm milk

Flour

Custard

Sugar

Egg yolks

Make custard. Combine egg yolks, sugar and flour in saucepan; stir in warm milk.

7

Cook over medium heat, stirring constantly until mixture thickens and boils. Boil and stir for 1 minute.

8

Vanilla

Remove from heat; let cool; then add vanilla.

9

Confectioners' sugar

Make a slash and fill fried puffs with custard. Sprinkle with confectioners' sugar.

41

Banana and Apple Fritters

Ingredients for 4 servings.
2 apples; 3 bananas.
For Batter:
1 egg yolk; 2 tablespoons sugar; 1/2 cup milk or water; 1 cup flour.
For Meringue:
1 egg white; 1 tablespoon sugar.
Confectioners' sugar. Oil or shortening for frying.

For Custard Sauce:
2 egg yolks; 3 tablespoons sugar; 1 teaspoon flour; 1 cup milk; Vanilla extract; Brandy.

1

Egg yolk
2 tablespoons sugar
Batter

Combine egg yolk and sugar in bowl to make batter. Mix well.

2

1/2 cup milk

Gradually stir in milk or water.

3

1 cup flour

Stir in sifted flour.

4

1 tablespoon sugar
Meringue
Egg white
Clean bowl

Make meringue. Beat egg white, adding sugar, until stiff. Fold meringue into flour mixture.

5

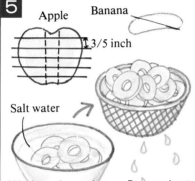

Apple
Banana
3/5 inch
Salt water

Wash apples and core. Pare and cut into 3/5 inch slices. Dip sliced apples in salt water and drain. Peel bananas and cut in half.

6

Batter
Fritter rises to top soon.
365°F
Oil

Heat oil to 365°F. Dip sliced apples and bananas into batter and fry.

7

Confectioners' sugar

Drain on paper towels. Sprinkle with confectioners' sugar.

8

3 tablespoons sugar
1 teaspoon flour
Custard sauce
Stir in 2 tablespoons warm milk.
Egg yolks
12 tablespoons warm milk

Make custard sauce. In saucepan, combine egg yolks, 2 tablespoons warm milk, sugar, and flour. Stir in 12 tablespoons warm milk and cook until smooth.

9

Vanilla
Brandy

Remove from heat, let cool. Add vanilla and brandy. Pour over hot fritters.

Doughnuts

Ingredients for 15 Doughnuts.
For Dough:
2 cups flour; 2 teaspoons baking powder; 3 tablespoons sugar; 3 tablespoons butter; 1 egg; 1/4 cup
milk.
For Topping:
Apricot jam; Chopped peanuts; Sliced chocolate;
1/2 cup confectioners' sugar and 2 teaspoons water
for icing; Confectioners' sugar.
Oil or shortening for frying.

Utensils

1

Sugar
Baking powder
Flour

Sift flour, baking powder, and sugar into bowl.

2

Beaten egg
Milk

Add egg and milk. Blend with hands.

3

Softened butter

Let butter warm to room temperature. Fold in softened butter with hands.

4

Knead lightly to make smooth dough.

5

Plastic bag
15 minutes

Put dough in a plastic bag and refrigerate for about 15 minutes to rest.

6 Roll out dough to 2/5 inch thickness and cut out using doughnut cutter.

Batter rises to top soon
365°F
Oil

Deep-fry cut-out dough, turning once, until golden brown on both sides.

7

Icing
B
Chocolate
(Mix confectioners' sugar with water)
A Peanuts
Jam

Drain on paper towels. For B, brush with icing and sprinkle with shredded chocolates. For A, brush with jam and sprinkle with chopped peanuts.

8

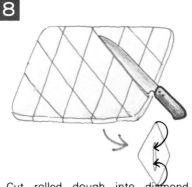

Cut rolled dough into diamond shapes. Make a slash in center. Put both ends in the slash and twist.

9

Deep-fry until done. Drain. Sprinkle with confectioners' sugar.

Crêpes

This fancy dessert is the traditional French pancake.
Try to make them paper-thin.

Variation

Ingredients for twelve 7-inch crêpes.
For Batter:
4/5 cup flour; 2 eggs; 1 cup milk; 8 teaspoons butter; 10 teaspoons sugar; Dash of salt.
Butter for cooking.
For Whipped Cream:
1 cup heavy cream; 10 teaspoons sugar; Vanilla extract; Brandy.
Custard (see page 41); Strawberries; Kiwi fruits.

Utensils

1

Salt   Flour
Sugar   Sifter

Sift flour, sugar, and salt in bowl. Make hollow and eggs in center.

2

Milk

Pour in milk and stir. If there are lumps, strain through a sieve.

3

Hot water
Melted butter

Melt butter, placing bowl in hot water. Stir in melted butter.

4

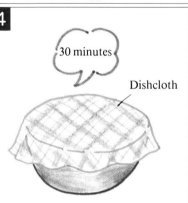

30 minutes
Dishcloth

Cover mixture with dishcloth and rest for about 30 minutes to blend well.

5

Butter

Heat skillet. Butter it and pour in a small amount of batter, turning pan to coat bottom.

6

Wax paper
Spatula

When it becomes light brown underneath, turn it and cook until light brown.

7

Brandy   Vanilla   Whipped cream
Sugar
Heavy cream
Ice water

Make whipped cream. Combine all ingredients for whipped cream in bowl and beat them, placing bowl in ice water.

8

Whipped cream
Custard

Spread crêpes with whipped cream or custard and the desired fruits. Fold or roll as you like.

Rolled Crêpes

Kiwi fruits
Strawberries

Make rolled crêpes filled with custard or whipped cream and fruits. Decorate tops with creams and fruits, too.

47

Pancakes

A

Use griddle or heavy skillet for smooth surface. Serve hot with whipped butter, maple syrup, jam, or yogurt.

Variation:

B

Ingredients for eight 4-inch pancakes. 2 eggs; 6 tablespoons sugar; 1 cup milk; 2 cups flour; 1 tablespoon baking powder; 3 tablespoons butter; Butter or margarine for cooking.

For Jams or Sauces:
A) Butter, honey, strawberry jam and apricot jam.
B) Whipped cream, candied cherries (red and green) and angelica.
C) Butter and chocolate sauce.

Utensils

1

Eggs

Beat eggs lightly in bowl.

2

Sugar

Add sugar and beat until foamy.

3

Milk

Gradually pour in milk and beat.

4

Flour and baking powder

Sift flour with baking powder. Fold sifted flour mixture into egg mixture.

5

Hot water

Melted butter

Fold melted butter into flour mixture.

6

Grease lightly

Heat heavy skillet over medium heat. Grease lightly. Pour small amount of batter into skillet.

7
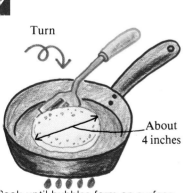

Turn

About 4 inches

Cook until bubbles form on surface. Turn and cook. Serve hot with butter, honey, or jam. Cut in half.

B

Arrange cut-cake as

Angelica

Candied cherries

Whipped cream

shown on serving dish. Garnish with whipped cream, candied cherries, and angelica.

C
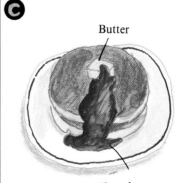

Butter

Chocolate sauce

Place cakes on serving dish. Place butter and chocolate sauce on top.

Ingredients for 10 Waffles.
For Batter:
2 eggs; 1/3 cup sugar; 2 teaspoons honey; 1 cup flour; 1/4 teaspoon baking powder; 5 tablespoons milk; Vanilla extract.
For Custard:
2 egg yolks; 1/3 cup sugar; 1 tablespoon flour; 1 tablespoon cornstarch. (See page 31 for directions.)
Oil for greasing waffle iron.

Utensils

1

Eggs

Beat eggs lightly in bowl.

2

Sugar | Honey

Add sugar and honey. Beat until foamy.

3

Baking powder | Flour

Fold in flour sifted with baking powder.

4

Vanilla

Milk

Stir in milk and vanilla.

5

Heat waffle iron and grease. Pour batter into waffle iron.

6

Fork

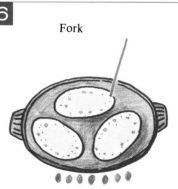

Cook until bubbles form on surface. Turn using fork.

7

Custard

See page 31 for making custard.

Place custard, fold in half.

Heart-shaped Waffles

Attach cord

Use heart-shaped waffle iron and cook. Attach golden cord to each waffle as shown.

Note:
About Oil for Deep-Fry Cakes.
Use salad oil or shortening for deep-frying cakes. They don't smell and they are light. Oil is apt to absorb odors, so don't use oil left from frying meats or vegetables to fry cakes.

Ingredients for 5 steamed apples.
apples; 1/2 cup granulated sugar; Dash of cinnamon;
tablespoons butter; 1-1/3 ounces raisins.
or Syrup:
tablespoons sugar; 1/2 cup water.

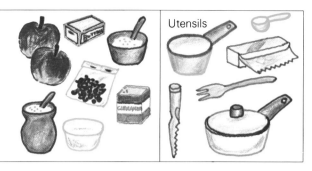

Utensils

1

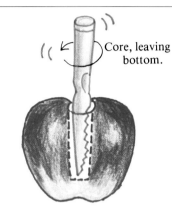

Core, leaving bottom.

Wash apples and core, leaving bottom.

2

Prick entire surface evenly with a fork to prevent it from bursting while steaming.

3

Granulated sugar

Butter

Raisins

Wash raisins in hot water.

Fill centers with granulated sugar, butter, cinnamon and raisins.

4

Syrup

Sugar

Water

Combine water and sugar in saucepan to make syrups. Heat. Let cool.

5

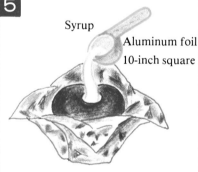

Syrup

Aluminum foil
10-inch square

Wrap each apple in aluminum foil and pour syrup into center. Close each top.

6

Cook for about 25 to 30 minutes.

Pour boiling water to one-third of apples.

Place wrapped apples in saucepan and pour boiling water to one-third of apples. Cook for about 25 to 30 minutes.

 Note:

When Your Cakes Fail.
Even though you did your best, sometimes you may have a miserable result. Try to use failed cakes: Cut them into small pieces. Soak them in brandy or rum and serve with whipped cream and fruits. Fry small pieces and sprinkle with confectioners' sugar or serve with jam. When you cannot use them, dry them in a slow oven and make crumbs to mix with batter or sprinkle over baked cakes.

This cake doesn't look good.

Serve with whipped cream and fruits.

Fry and sprinkle with confectioners' sugar or serve with jam.

Soak in brandy or rum.

Fruit Cocktail with Junket

Ingredients for 5-6 servings.
1 block agar and 1-1/4 cups water; 2/3 cup sugar;
1 cup milk; Vanilla extract;
Fruits in season (Cherries, Kiwi, Mandarin oranges,
Pineapple).
For syrup:
5/6 cup sugar; 1 tablespoon lemon juice; 1-1/2
cups water; 1 tablespoon liqueur.

Utensils

1

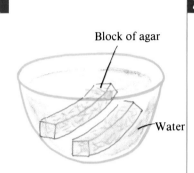

Block of agar

Water

Wash block of agar and soak it in water for more than 30 minutes.

2

1-1/4 cups water

Squeezed agar

Drain water and squeeze agar. Tear agar into small pieces. Place them with water in saucepan and heat.

3

3/4 cup sugar

After boiling, add sugar

Liquid agar

Heat to boiling, then add sugar. Stir to dissolve sugar.

4

Strain through a sieve after agar and sugar are dissolved. Cook for 1 to 2 minutes more.

5

Milk

Vanilla

Remove from heat. Let cool. Add milk and vanilla.

6

Pour into square pan and refrigerate.

7

5/6 cup sugar

Syrup

1-1/2 cups water

Liqueur

Lemon Juice

After cool, refrigerate.

Combine sugar and water in saucepan to make syrups. Heat to dissolve sugar. Remove from heat. Let cool. Add lemon juice and brandy.

8

Pineapple

Cherries

Mandarins

Kiwi fruit

Syrup

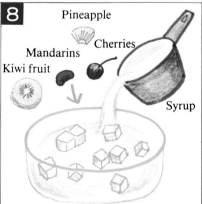

Place diced junket and fruits in bowl and pour syrup over.

Note:
About Agar and Gelatin.
Block of Agar, made from seaweed is carbohydrate. Agar does not have any nutritious value but becomes firm at room temperature and is palatable. It is often used to make Japanese sweets. Gelatin, made from bones or skins of animals, has protein and becomes firm at 70°F. It is often used to make cold desserts because of its transparency and resilience.

Compote

A

Variations:

B

Use fruits in season and select a harmony of colors, placing them in attractive serving dishes.

Ingredients for 4 servings.
tart apples; 10 dried plums.
syrup (5/6 cup sugar and 1-1/2 cups water); 2 tablespoons lemon juice; 1/2 cup white wine.
desired fruits (Cherries, Mandarin oranges, and
strawberries).
cinnamon sticks; Whipped cream.

Utensils

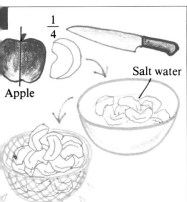

Apple

Salt water

1/4

Cut apples into quarters, pare, and core. Dip them in salt water and drain immediately.

2

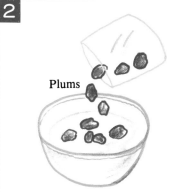

Plums

Soak dried plums in water.

3

Apples

Plums

Sugar and water

Combine sugar and water in saucepan. Heat. Make syrup and add apples and plums. Cook for about 15 minutes.

Lemon juice

When almost done, add lemon juice and cook until tender.

5

White wine

Remove from heat, add white wine and let cool. Refrigerate to chill.

6

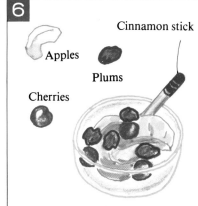

Cinnamon stick

Apples

Plums

Cherries

Place on serving dish. Garnish with cherries and mandarins.

A

1/2

Mandarins

Whipped cream

Cherries

Core and pare apple. Cut across apple in half. Cook in same way as above. Garnish with whipped cream, cherries and mandarins.

B

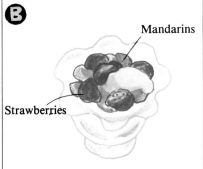

Mandarins

Strawberries

Garnish with mandarins and strawberries.

Bananas Flambé

Bananas Flambé

Variation:

Cherries Flambé

Use fresh or canned cherries. Also, try flambéed pineapple or sliced apples. They are really dramatic desserts.

Bananas Flambé

Ingredients for 2-3 servings.

3 bananas; 2 tablespoons butter; 3 tablespoons granulated sugar; 2 teaspoons lemon juice; 1/2 cup orange juice; Brandy.

For Cherries Flambé:

Ingredients (2-3 servings) 1 can cherries; 2 tablespoons butter; 3 tablespoons granulated sugar; 2 teaspoons lemon juice; 1/2 cup red wine; Brandy.

1

Granulated sugar

Butter

Heat skillet and melt butter. Add granulated sugar.

2

Lemon juice

Stir with a fork and brown sugar lightly. Add lemon juice.

3

Peel bananas and cut in half. Place them in skillet and brown both sides lightly.

4

Orange juice

Pour orange juice over bananas and cook until juice is thickened.

5

Brandy

Pour brandy over bananas the instant before removing from heat. Ignite and spoon juices over fruits until flame dies.

Note:

Tips for Beating Eggs.

Use bowl and wire whisk as big as possible for quick beating.

To beat whole eggs: Stir eggs gently, then beat vigorously with up and down motions, trapping as much air as possible. If you take a rest for a long time while beating, air may be lost and lose durability. When stiff peaks do not form in spite of beating for a long time, place bowl in warm water and beat more. To beat egg whites: Use clean and dry bowl free from grease or water. Stir egg whites gently, then beat until foamy. Add sugar and flavors after whites are well beaten.

For Cherries Flambé

Cherries

Butter
Granulated sugar
Lemon juice

Follow steps 1 and 2. Place cherries skillet. Pour in lemon juice.

Red wine

Add brandy

2

Pour red wine over cherries and cook until wine is thickened. Add brandy as above.

Mashed Sweet Potatoes

Ingredients for 20 Mashed Sweet Potatoes. 1-2/3 pounds sweet potatoes including skins (1 pound when mashed); 5/6 cup sugar; 1 egg yolk; Vanilla extract.

For Topping:
Confectioners' sugar for A; Cinnamon for B; Powdered green tea and walnuts for C; Sliced almonds and candied cherries for D.

Utensils

1

4/5 inch

Water

Soak about 30 minutes

Wash sweet potatoes and cut them into 4/5 inch slices. Pare thickly and soak in water for about 30 minutes.

2

Place slices on a rack in a hot steamer with boiling water and steam until tender.

3

Strain through a sieve while they are warm. Make 1 pound mashed sweet potatoes.

4

Sugar

Combine mashed sweet potatoes and sugar in saucepan.

5

Cook, stirring constantly until smooth. Remove from heat and let cool.

6

Egg yolk

Vanilla

Add egg yolk and vanilla. Shape into balls or ovals. (See step 8 for C.)

7

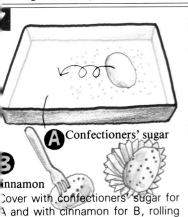

Ⓐ Confectioners' sugar

Ⓑ Cinnamon

Cover with confectioners' sugar for A and with cinnamon for B, rolling shaped potatoes over sugar or cinnamon.

8

Ⓒ

Powdered green tea

Walnuts

Dissolve powdered green tea in hot water; mix with mashed sweet potatoes. Shape into balls. Garnish with walnuts.

9

Ⓓ Chopped almonds

Cherries

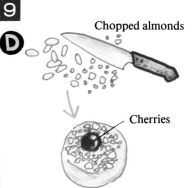

Garnish with cherries and chopped almonds.

Chocolate Fudge

Ingredients for 15 pieces of Chocolate Fudge.
1 cup sweet chocolate; 2/5 cup heavy cream; Vanilla extract; Liqueur.
For A: Marzipan (hearts)
For B: Cocoa
For C: Confectioners' sugar
For D: Slivered and toasted almonds

Utensils

1

Shred chocolate.

2

Heavy cream

Place heavy cream in saucepan and heat until bubbles form.

3

Remove from heat. Add shred chocolate and stir to melt.

4

Turn chocolate mixture into bowl.

Vanilla
Brandy

2/5 inch diameter round tip

Add vanilla and liqueur. Let cool. Turn into pastry bag with 2/5 inch diameter round tip.

5 Squeeze into small aluminum cups.

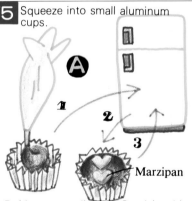

A

1
2
3

Marzipan

Refrigerate until firm. Garnish with marzipan hearts and return to refrigerator.

6

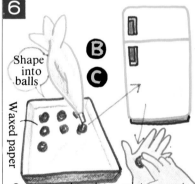

Shape into balls

B
C

Waxed paper

Squeeze chocolate mixture onto waxed paper. Refrigerate. Remove from refrigerator and shape into balls with hands.

7

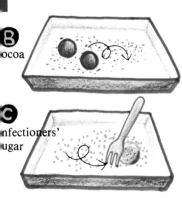

B Cocoa

C Confectioners' sugar

Roll shaped fudges over cocoa for B and confectioners' sugar for C.

8

Slivered and toasted almonds

D

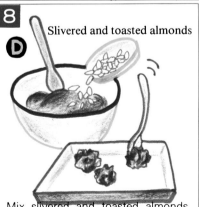

Mix slivered and toasted almonds with chocolate mixture. Spoon onto pan and refrigerate.

How to Serve Cakes and Entertain

About Serving Dishes:
★ Use dishes bigger than cakes.

Place lace papers on serving dishes.

★ Use colorful dishes for plain cakes.

★ Use plain dishes for decorated cakes.

To slice cake:
★ Warm knife before slicing cakes.

To place fork:
Place fork on the far side of plate.

To serve cold desserts:
Use glass dishes.

★ Cool dishes before using.

Let's invite your friends!

About Tea Party:
★ Tea goes well with cakes. When you serve coffee, brew it strong. Japanese tea also goes with cakes.

Decorate with flowers.

For Gifts:
★ Make Butter Cakes, Marble cakes, or Chocolate Fudge for gifts.

After completely cool, wrap cakes.

Butter Cake

★ Use an elegant tablecloth made of a lace or flower pattern.

★ Prepare plenty of plates, knives, and forks.

Seal

Attach card written with the recipe and origin of the cake.

Cellophane

Ribbon